PIANO/VOCAL SELECTIONS

A NEW MUSICAL
WICKED

MUSIC & LYRICS BY STEPHEN SCHWARTZ

Marc Platt
Universal Pictures
The Araca Group   and   Jon B. Platt
David Stone
present

Idina Menzel

Kristin Chenoweth

WICKED

Music and Lyrics   Book
Stephen Schwartz   **Winnie Holzman**

Based on the novel by Gregory Maguire

Also Starring

Carole Shelley
Norbert Leo Butz

Michelle Federer   Christopher Fitzgerald   William Youmans

Ioana Alfonso   Ben Cameron   Cristy Candler   Kristy Cates   Melissa Bell Chait   Marcus Choi
Kristoffer Cusick   Kathy Deitch   Melissa Fahn   Rhett G. George   Kristen Leigh Gorski   Manuel Herrera
Kisha Howard   LJ Jellison   Sean McCourt   Corinne McFadden   Mark Myars   Jan Neuberger
Walter Winston ONeil   Andrew Palermo   Andy Pellick   Michael Seelbach   Lorna Ventura   Derrick Williams

and

Joel Grey
as the Wizard

Settings	Costumes	Lighting	Sound
Eugene Lee	**Susan Hilferty**	**Kenneth Posner**	**Tony Meola**
Projections	Wigs & Hair	Production Supervisor	Technical Supervisor
Elaine J. McCarthy	**Tom Watson**	**Steven Beckler**	**Jake Bell**
Music Arrangements		Dance Arrangements	Music Coordinator
Alex Lacamoire & Stephen Oremus		**James Lynn Abbott**	**Michael Keller**
Associate Set Designer	Special Effects	Flying Sequences	Assistant Director
Edward Pierce	**Chic Silber**	**Paul Rubin/ZFX, Inc.**	**Lisa Leguillou**
Casting	Marketing	General Management	Press	Executive Producers
Bernard Telsey Casting	**TMG - The Marketing Group**	**EGS**	**The Publicity Office**	**Marcia Goldberg & Nina Essman**

Orchestrations
William David Brohn

Music Director
Stephen Oremus

Musical Staging by
Wayne Cilento

Directed by
Joe Mantello

Original Broadway Company

www.stephenschwartz.com

Photos by Joan Marcus

ISBN 0-634-07881-X

HAL•LEONARD®
CORPORATION
7777 W. BLUEMOUND RD. P.O. BOX 13819 MILWAUKEE, WI 53213

In Australia Contact:
Hal Leonard Australia Pty. Ltd.
22 Taunton Drive   P.O. Box 5130
Cheltenham East, 3192   Victoria, Australia
Email: ausadmin@halleonard.com

Visit Hal Leonard Online at
www.halleonard.com

CONTENTS

Top Left – Joel Grey
Top Right – Norbert Leo Butz
Bottom Left – Idina Menzel & Kristin Chenoweth
Bottom Right – Kristin Chenoweth

Idina Menzel

Note from the Composer

Several decisions always have to be made in translating the score from a show into a book of vocal selections. In the case of *Wicked*, I found it trickier than usual, because many of the songs are structured to carry the story in the show, but out-of-context would be clearer and more effective to perform in a somewhat altered format.

In the end, I chose to try to make the songs work for this medium, and thus to make changes in certain cases from the way they appear in the stage show and on the cast album. This entailed writing new lyrics in some instances ("No One Mourns the Wicked" and "Defying Gravity"), providing new endings for some of the songs ("Dancing Through Life", "Defying Gravity", "Wonderful"), and eliminating interior chorus sections, intros, or other show-oriented material from several of the selections. In addition, I excerpted one section of the opening of Act Two to create a separate song, "I Couldn't Be Happier." Two of the songs appear in the book, as in the show, as duets— "As Long as You're Mine" and "For Good" —but of course, either can be performed as a solo.

(In special circumstances, when someone needs a song in the original show format, that can be obtained by emailing me at **schwartz@stephenschwartz.com**. But it seemed to me that for most people and purposes, these changes would be preferable.)

The piano accompaniment is essentially a reduction of what is played by the show orchestra, although some adjustments were necessary to accommodate the vocal line. Those interested in having the vocal line and a separate piano accompaniment should see the *Vocal Selections* version of this book.

The chord symbols used should be relatively familiar to anyone accustomed to reading such symbols, but a few specific explanations are probably in order:

C5 means a C chord with no 3rd (CG)

Csus2 means a C chord with a 2nd rather than a 3rd (CDG)

C(add 9) means a C major chord plus the 2nd or 9th (CDEG)

C(add 4) means a C major chord plus the 4th (CEFG)

I want to acknowledge the help of Alex Lacamoire, Stephen Oremus and Mark Carlstein in preparing and editing this music, so that this book can be as clear, thorough, and accurate as possible.

I hope you enjoy it.

Stephen Schwartz

NO ONE MOURNS THE WICKED

Music and Lyrics by
STEPHEN SCHWARTZ

Flowing, not too slow

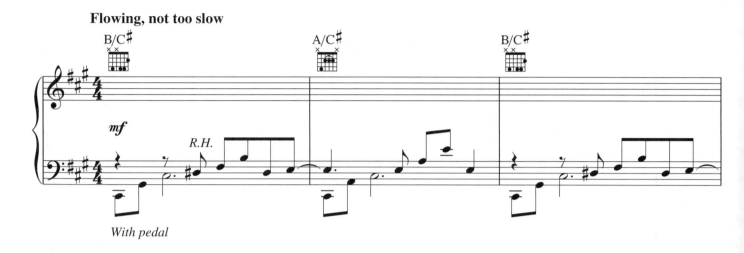

With pedal

No one mourns the wick-ed! _____

No one cries: "They won't re - turn!" No one lays a

THE WIZARD AND I

Music and Lyrics by
STEPHEN SCHWARTZ

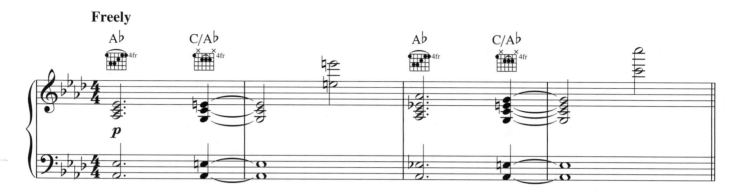

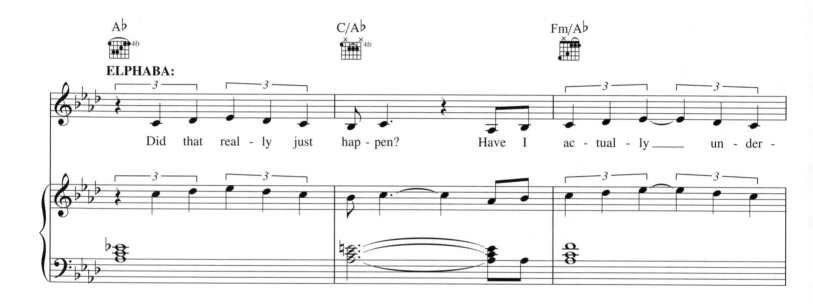

ELPHABA:
Did that real-ly just hap-pen? Have I ac-tual-ly_____ un-der-

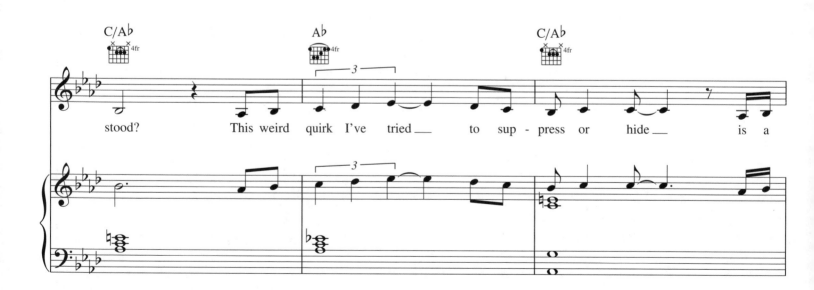

stood? This weird quirk I've tried____ to sup-press or hide____ is a

WHAT IS THIS FEELING?

Music and Lyrics by
STEPHEN SCHWARTZ

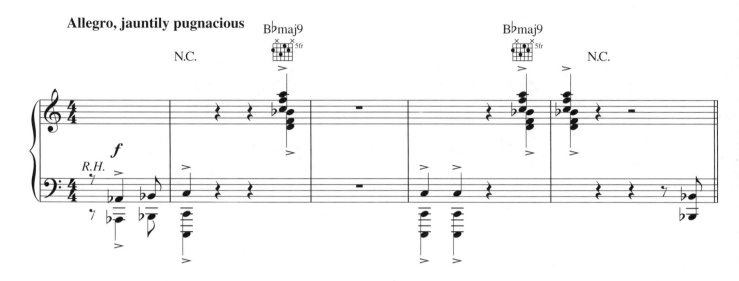

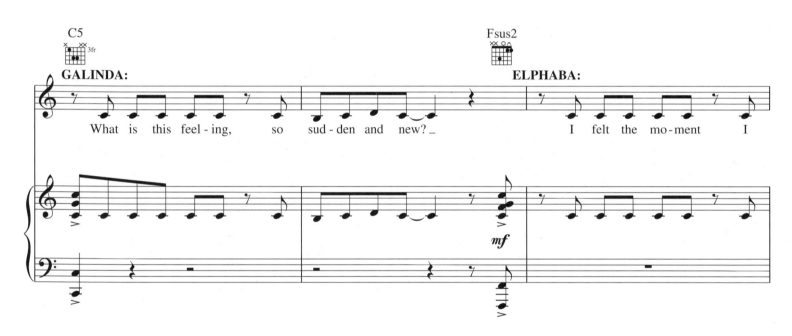

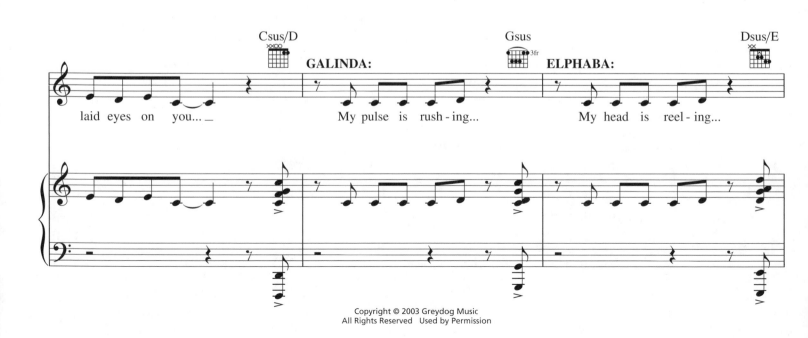

34

DANCING THROUGH LIFE

Music and Lyrics by
STEPHEN SCHWARTZ

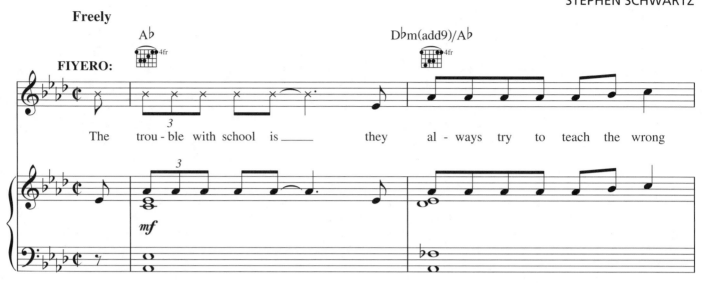

you'll be hap - py to be ___ there... ___

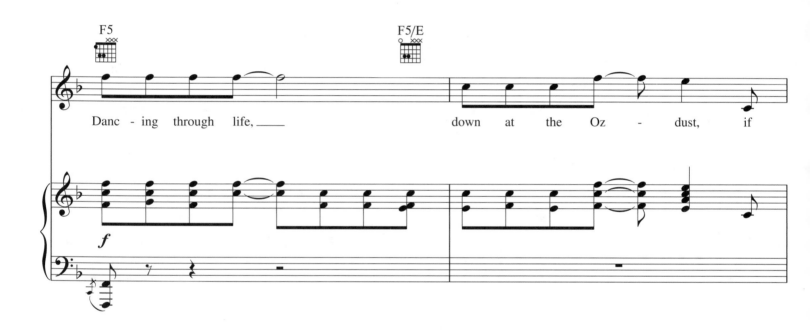

Danc - ing through life, ___ down at the Oz - dust, if

on - ly be - cause ___ dust is what we come to... ___ Noth - ing mat - ters but

Top – Idina Menzel & Kristin Chenoweth
Bottom – Christopher Fitzgerald & Michelle Federer

Someone Like You

—Adele '11

I heard that you're settled down
That you found a girl and you're married now
I heard that your dreams came true
Guess she gave you things I didn't give to you
Old friend, why are you so shy?
Ain't like you to hold back or hide from the light

I hate to turn up out of the blue uninvited
But I couldn't stay away, I couldn't fight it
I had hoped you'd see my face
And that you'd be reminded that for me it isn't over

Never mind, I'll find someone like you
I wish nothing but the best for you too
Don't forget me, I beg, I remember you said
Sometimes it lasts in love but sometimes it hurts instead
Sometimes it lasts in love but sometimes it hurts instead
Yeah

You know how the time flies
Only yesterday was the time of our lives
We were born and raised in a summer haze
Bound by the surprise of our glory days

POPULAR

Music and Lyrics by
STEPHEN SCHWARTZ

When-ev-er I see some-one less for-tu-nate than I— and let's face it, who is-n't less for-tu-nate than I? —My ten-der heart tends to start to bleed And when some-one needs a make-o-ver, I sim-ply have to take o-ver; I

I'M NOT THAT GIRL

Music and Lyrics by
STEPHEN SCHWARTZ

Simple and steady, like a music box

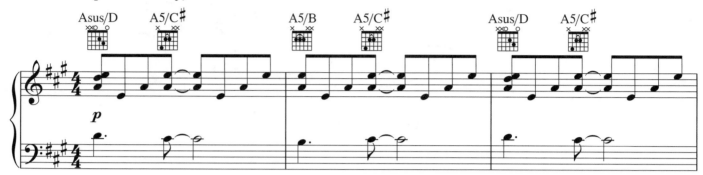

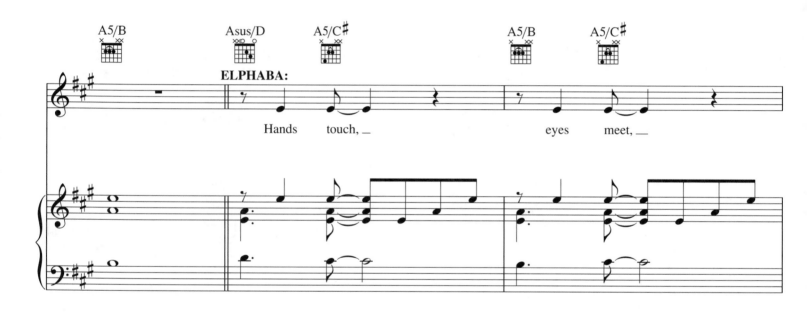

ELPHABA:

Hands touch, __ eyes meet, __

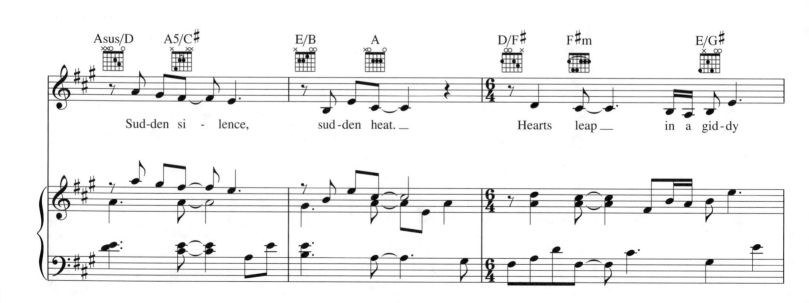

Sud-den si - lence, sud-den heat. __ Hearts leap __ in a gid-dy

Carole Shelley & Joel Grey

ONE SHORT DAY

Music and Lyrics by
STEPHEN SCHWARTZ

Freely, sung almost in a whisper

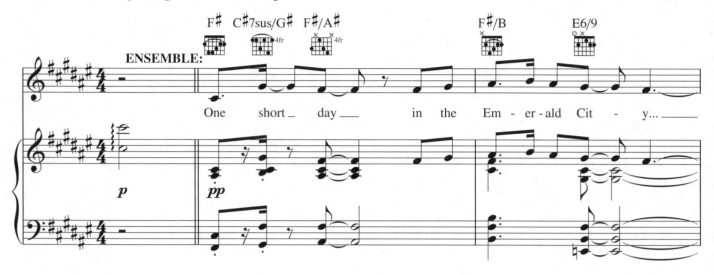

ENSEMBLE:

One short day in the Em-er-ald Cit-y...

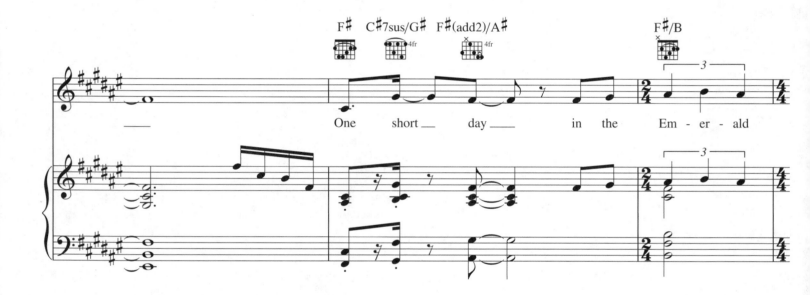

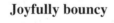

One short day in the Em-er-ald

Joyfully bouncy

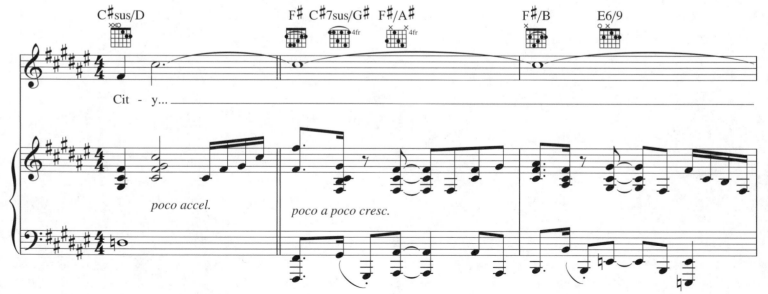

Cit-y...

poco accel.

poco a poco cresc.

63

DEFYING GRAVITY

Music and Lyrics by
STEPHEN SCHWARTZ

Freely, with quiet intensity

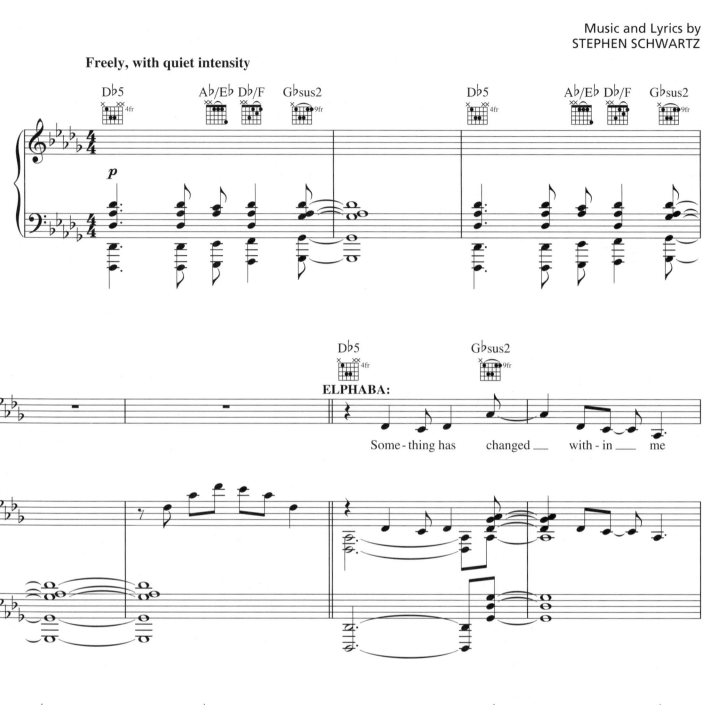

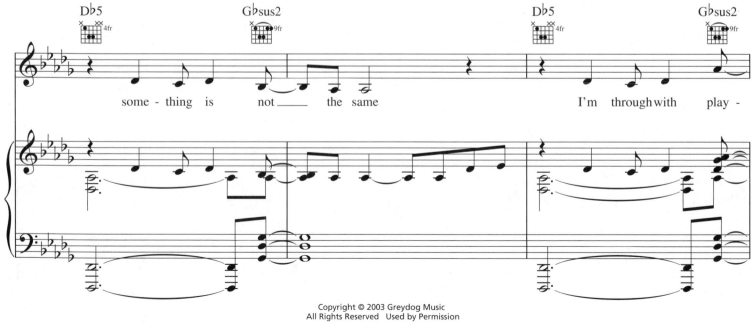

I COULDN'T BE HAPPIER

Music and Lyrics by
STEPHEN SCHWARTZ

WONDERFUL

Music and Lyrics by
STEPHEN SCHWARTZ

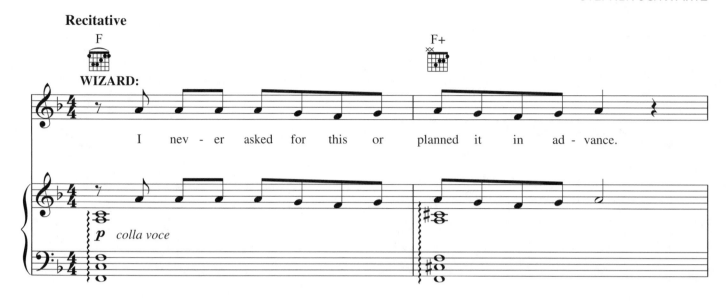

Recitative

WIZARD:

I nev-er asked for this or planned it in ad-vance.

p colla voce

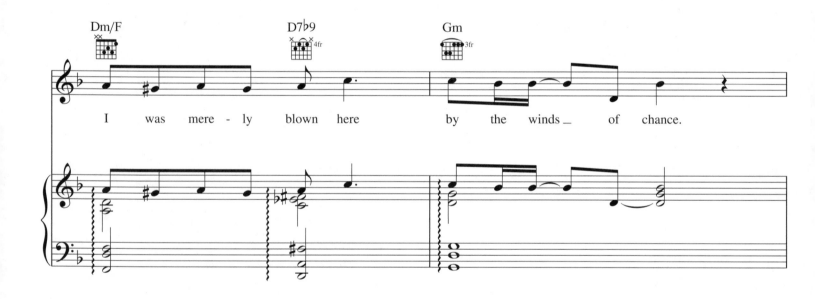

I was mere-ly blown here by the winds ___ of chance.

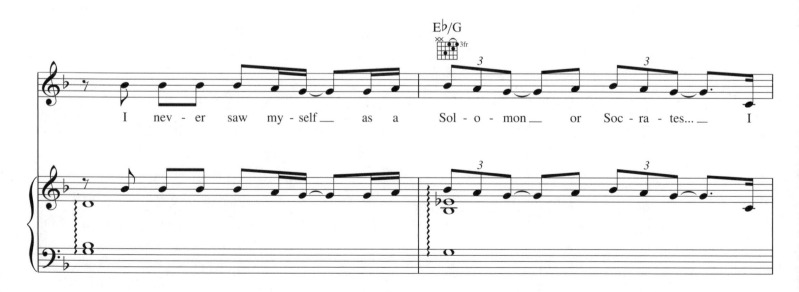

I nev-er saw my-self ___ as a Sol-o-mon ___ or Soc-ra-tes... ___ I

Where I come from, we believe all sorts of things that aren't true—we call it..."history."

rall.

A

Soft-shoe (♩♩ = ♩ ♪)

man's called a trai - tor   or lib - er - a - tor;   A

rich man's a thief   or phi - lan - thro - pist.   Is

one a cru - sad - er   or ruth - less in - vad - er?   It's

AS LONG AS YOU'RE MINE

Music and Lyrics by
STEPHEN SCHWARTZ

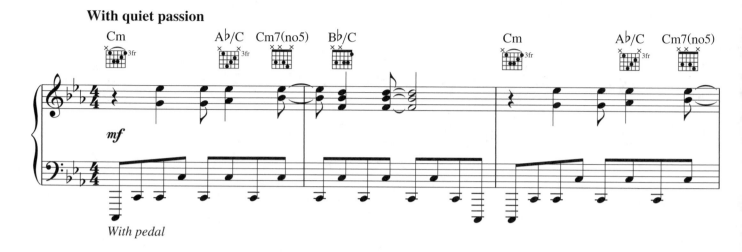

as long as you're _____ mine... _____

Joel Grey & Idina Menzel

NO GOOD DEED

Music and Lyrics by
STEPHEN SCHWARTZ

FOR GOOD

Music and Lyrics by
STEPHEN SCHWARTZ

Note: When performed as a solo, sing the top melody line throughout.

Tenderly, poco rubato

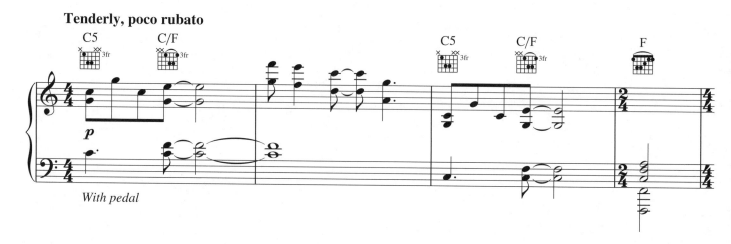

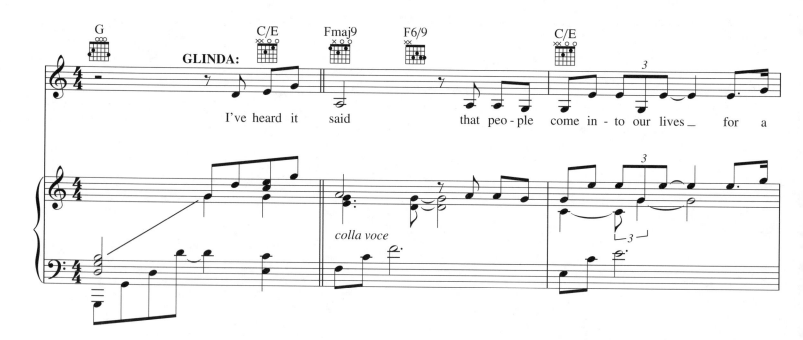

GLINDA:

I've heard it said that peo-ple come in-to our lives _ for a

rea - son, bring-ing some -thing we must learn. And we are led to those who

114